How to Build a Beautiful Wardrobe on a Budget
Children's Fashion Books

BABY PROFESSOR
EDUCATION KIDS

Speedy Publishing LLC
40 E. Main St. #1156
Newark, DE 19711
www.speedypublishing.com

Building a beautiful wardrobe is not hard when you have an unlimited clothing budget that lets you shop til you drop and come out at the end with tons of clothes you love.

However, when you have a limited budget, building a wardrobe that you love and enjoy wearing takes a little some planning.

Nothing on a budget ever comes easy, except for maybe ramen noodles. In the end, however, having a closet of clothes that you love that is within your budget is worth the effort.

A budget wardrobe you love is possible. Here's how:

Have a Plan.

Step 1: create a budget. Consider how much you can spend for clothes each month.

Step 2: Make a plan for shopping. Consider the basics that you would like to add to the wardrobe and make sure to write those down.

Once you have your budget and your shopping list, you can build your budget wardrobe bit by bit. It will take patience, but you will be surprised at how your wardrobe grows.

Shop in your closet. Before you go to the stores, shop first in your closet. Check for what you already have that can serve your purposes in making the wardrobe.

There's a chance that you have more than you think. Clear things out so you can clearly see what you have. Give away the clothes you have outgrown or never wear.

Once you have cleared out the clothes that you don't love from your closet, you can better see what you need to do. Compare what you already have to your shopping list and consider what you really need to get right away.

Try second
hand items.

You can still find good quality clothing and accessories in second-hand shops. They are a lot cheaper than what you see in the mall.

It just takes a little more time and effort to select the good pieces from all the clothing you see in those second-hand shops. Check for stains, for rips, and for worn-out places.

Don't buy clothes and accessories you are not certain to wear.

When you buy things that you will not wear, even if your favorite singer wears the same thing, you are just wasting your money.

Determine what you really like to wear so you won't spend on stuff that will end up hidden in your closet.

If you choose to try out a style you are not sure of, save the receipts and don't clip the tags until you are sure that you will commit to wear these things. Return anything you don't absolutely love.

These are just
a few ideas of
how you can
build a beautiful
wardrobe on
a budget.

Visit

BABY PROFESSOR
EDUCATION KIDS

www.BabyProfessorBooks.com

to download Free Baby Professor eBooks
and view our catalog of new and exciting
Children's Books

CPSIA information can be obtained
at www.ICGtesting.com
Printed in the USA
LVHW060727171222
735213LV00009BA/1227